TABLE OF CONTENTS

I0427905

ACRONYMS

ACLU	American Civil Liberties Union
CTRC	Citizen Targeting Review Court
FISC	Foreign Intelligence Surveillance Court
ICRC	International Committee of the Red Cross
NSC	National Security Court
SROEs	Standing Rules of Engagement
U.S.	United States

CHAPTER 1

INTRODUCTION

No person shall be held to answer for a capital, or otherwise infamous crime, unless on a presentment or indictment of a Grand Jury . . . nor be deprived of life, liberty, or property, without due process of law.

— Amendment V, *U.S. Constitution*

Don't consult with anybody in the killing of Americans. Fighting the devil doesn't require consultation or prayer seeking divine guidance. They are the party of the devils. Fighting them is what is called for at this time. We have reached a point where it is either us or them. We are two opposites that will never come together. What they want can only be accomplished by our elimination. Therefore, this is a defining battle.

— Anwar al-Awlaki, YouTube

Anwar al-Awlaki was a United States (U.S.) citizen.[1] Al-Awlaki was born in New Mexico[2] and went to college in Colorado.[3] Although he lived in Yemen, al-Awlaki never renounced his U.S. citizenship.[4] Although known principally a propagandist who delivered anti-American sermons in English, and posted internet videos supporting al-Qaeda, he was suspected of having taken on more of an operational role within al-Qaeda in the Arabian Peninsula.[5] Al-Awlaki was linked to the Fort Hood shooter, Major Nidal Hasan, with whom he exchanged emails, and was suspected of recruiting and training Umar Farouk Abdulmutallab, the Christmas Day bomber who attempted to bring down Northwest Airlines Flight 253 with explosive laced underwear.[6]

Around January 2010, al-Awlaki was added to the "capture or kill" list maintained by the U.S. military's Joint Special Operations Command.[7] An intelligence memorandum leaked from the Obama Administration concluded that it would be legal to kill al-Awlaki, because he posed a threat to the U.S., if Yemeni authorities were

1

unwilling or unable to stop him, and capture proved infeasible.[8] However, he was never

publically indicted by the government for any crime.[9]

In *Al-Aulaqi v. Obama*, Anwar al-Awlaki's father, Nasser al-Aulaqi[1] sued the

President of the United States, the Secretary of Defense, and the Director of the Central

Intelligence Agency, in the United States District Court for the District of Columbia

(collectively "defendants").[10] Al-Awlaki's father claimed the defendants violated his

son's Fourth Amendment right to freedom from unreasonable seizures and his son's Fifth

Amendment right not to be deprived of life without due process.[11] Al-Awlaki's father

also claimed the defendants violated the Fifth Amendment's Due Process Clause by

refusing to disclose the criteria by which the U.S. selects citizens for targeted killing.

Finally, al-Awlaki's father claimed the defendants' targeted killings policy violated treaty

and customary international law.[12]

Al-Awlaki's father sought both declaratory and injunctive relief.[13] Al-Aulaqi

requested a declaration stating that the Constitution prohibited targeted killings of

American citizens, unless they presented a concrete, specific, and imminent threat to life

or physical safety, and no other means could reasonably be employed to neutralize that

threat.[14] Al-Aulaqi also requested a declaration stating that outside of armed-conflict,

treaty and customary international law prohibited targeted killing of individuals,

regardless of citizenship, again except where the individual presented a concrete, specific,

and imminent threat to life or physical safety, and no other means could reasonably be

---

[1]Anwar al-Awlaki used a different transliteration of his name from Arabic than
his father. However, this paper recognizes that other legal scholars may not have
recognized the distinction and therefore, when using direct quotations, retains the original
author's spelling, followed by "[sic]" where applicable.

employed to neutralize that threat.[15] Finally, al-Aulaqi requested a preliminary injunction prohibiting the defendants from killing his son.[16]

The defendants motioned to dismiss on grounds that al-Aulaqi lacked standing, failed to state a claim upon which relief could be granted, and presented nonjusticiable political questions.[17] The court agreed with the defendants that al-Aulaqi lacked standing.[18] The court also agreed with the defendants that al-Aulaqi failed to state a claim upon which relief could be granted.[19] Finally, the court agreed with the defendants that al-Aulaqi presented nonjusticiable political questions.[20] The court explained the political question doctrine "excludes from judicial review those controversies which revolve around policy choices and value determinations constitutionally committed for resolution to the halls of Congress or the confines of the Executive Branch."[21] The court also noted six factors articulated by the Supreme Court in determining whether a controversy poses a nonjusticiable political question:

> [1] a textually demonstrable constitutional commitment of the issue to a coordinate political department; or [2] a lack of judicially discoverable and manageable standards for resolving it; or [3] the impossibility of deciding without an initial policy determination of a kind clearly for nonjudicial discretion; or [4] the impossibility of a court's undertaking independent resolution without expressing lack of respect due coordinate branches of government; or [5] an unusual need for unquestioning adherence to a political decision already made; or [6] the potentiality of embarrassment from multifarious pronouncements by various departments on one question.[22]

The court noted the first two factors are considered the most important.[23] Additionally, a court need only conclude the presence of one factor for a case to be nonjusticiable, not all.[24] The court described national security, military matters, and foreign relations as quintessential sources for political questions.[25] Accordingly, the court granted the defendants' motion to dismiss the case.[26]

3

On 30 September 2011, Anwar al-Awlaki was killed in Yemen by a missile fired from an armed drone.[27] He was killed in a car carrying him and other top operatives from al-Qaeda in the Arabian Peninsula.[28] Among those killed was Samir Khan, another U.S. citizen, of Pakistani origin, who had grown up in Queens and North Carolina, and ran the group's English-language Internet magazine.[29] He had proclaimed that he was "proud to be a traitor to America."[30] Khan notoriously published articles with titles such as "Make a Bomb in the Kitchen of Your Mom."[31]

On 5 March 2012, in a speech at Northwestern University School of Law, Attorney General Eric Holder explained "United States citizenship alone does not make such individuals [like al-Awlaki] immune from being targeted."[32] Although Attorney General Holder recognized the Fifth Amendment's Due Process Clause precluded the government from depriving citizens of their lives without due process of law, he argued:

> [A]n operation using lethal force in a foreign country, targeted against a U.S. citizen who is a senior operational leader of al-Qaeda or associated forces, and who is actively engaged in planning to kill Americans, would be lawful at least in the following circumstances: First, the U.S. government has determined, after a thorough and careful review, that the individual poses an imminent threat of violent attack against the United States; second, capture is not feasible; and third, the operation would be conducted in a manner consistent with applicable law of war principles.[33]

Attorney General Holder asserted that the President is not required to get permission from any federal court before taking action against a U.S. citizen.[34] He explained that "'Due process' and 'judicial process' are not one and the same, particularly when it comes to national security."[35] He further explained that "The Constitution guarantees due process, not judicial process."[36] He stated that the Constitution's guarantee of due process "does not require judicial approval before the President may use force abroad against a senior operational leader of a foreign terrorist

4

organization with which the United States is at war–even if that individual happens to be a U.S. citizen."[37]

On 18 July 2012, Nasser al-Aulaqi, in his capacity as the personal representative of the estate of his son, Anwar al-Awlaki, and Sarah Khan, in her capacity as the personal representative of the estate of her son, Samir Khan, (collectively "plaintiffs") filed a complaint against Leon C. Panetta, in his official capacity as the Secretary of Defense, William H. McRaven, in his official capacity as the Commander, U.S. Special Operations Command, Joseph Votel, in his official capacity as Commander, Joint Special Operations Command, and David H. Petraeus, in his official capacity as Director, Central Intelligence Agency (collectively "defendants"), in the United States District Court for the District of Columbia.[38] The plaintiffs alleged that the defendants authorized and directed the killings of Anwar al-Awlaki and Samir Khan in Yemen on 30 September 2011.[39] They claimed that by directing their subordinates to fire upon al-Awlaki's vehicle, the defendants violated al-Awlaki and Khan's right to not be deprived of life without due process of law.[40] The plaintiffs noted that at the time of the killings, the U.S. was not engaged in armed-conflict with or within Yemen.[41] They asserted that "Outside the context of armed-conflict, both the United States Constitution and international human rights law prohibit the use of lethal force unless, at the time it is applied, lethal force is a last resort to protect against a concrete, specific, and imminent threat of death or serious physical injury."[42] The plaintiffs maintained that at the time of their killing, neither al-Awlaki nor Khan was engaged in activities posing any such threat, nor directly participating in hostilities within the meaning of the law of war.[43] The plaintiffs claimed that the killings of al-Awlaki and Khan were unlawful violations of their right to due process under the Fifth Amendment, their right to be free from unreasonable seizures under the Fourth Amendment, and their right to be free from legislation declaring them guilty of a crime without trial under the Bill of Attainder Clause.[44] The plaintiffs sought money damages from the defendants because they claimed that the deaths al-Awlaki and Khan were foreseeable consequences of the actions and omissions of the defendants.[45]

On 6 September 2012, President Barack Obama set out five rules for targeted killings.[46] He stated the targeting must be authorized by our laws, against a threat that is serious and not speculative, where the individual targeted cannot be captured before acting on that threat, avoid civilian casualties, and in the case of U.S. citizens, are subject to the protections of the Constitution and due process.

---

[1]Scott Shane, "U.S. Approves Targeted Killing of American Cleric," *New York Times*, 6 April 2010, A12.

[2]Ibid.

[3]J. M. Berger, "The Myth of Anwar al-Awlaki," *Foreign Policy*, 10 August 2011, http://www.foreignpolicy.com/articles/2011/08/10/the_myth_of_anwar_al_awlaki (accessed 29 November 2012).

[4]Peter Spiro, "al-Awlaki and Citizenship," *Opinio Juris*, 3 October 2011, http://opiniojuris.org/2011/10/03/al-awlaki-and-citizenship/ (accessed 29 November 2012).

[5]*PBS NewsHour*, PBS television broadcast, 30 September 2011, http://www.pbs.org/newshour/bb/terrorism/july-dec11/awlaki1_09-30.html (accessed 29 November 2012).

[6]Ibid.

[7]Dana Priest, "U.S. Military Teams, Intelligence Deeply Involved in aiding Yemen on Strikes," *Washington Post*, 27 January 2010, A01.

[8]Charlie Savage, "Secret U.S. Memo Made Legal Case to Kill a Citizen," *New York Times*, 6 October 2010, A1.

[9]*Al-Aulaqi v. Panetta*, Complaint 10, No. 12-cv-01192, United States District Court for the District of Columbia, 2012.

[10]*Al-Aulaqi v. Obama*, 727 F.Supp.2d 1, 8-54 (D.D.C. 2010).

[11]Ibid., 12.

[12]Ibid.

[13]Ibid.

[14]Ibid.

[15]Ibid.

[16]Ibid.

[17]Ibid., 13.

[18]Ibid., 35.

[19]Ibid.

[20]Ibid., 46.

[21]Ibid., 44.

[22]Ibid.

[23]Ibid.

[24]Ibid., 45.

[25]Ibid.

[26]Ibid., 54.

[27]Mark Mazetti, Eric Schmitt, and Robert F. Worth, "Two Year Manhunt Led to Killing of Al-Awlaki in Yemen," *New York Times*, 1 October 2011, A1.

[28]Ibid.

[29]Ibid.

[30]Ibid.

[31]Ibid.

[32]Justice News, "Attorney General Eric Holder Speaks at Northwestern University School of Law" (Chicago, 5 March 2012), http://www.justice.gov/iso/opa/ag/speeches/2012/ag-speech-1203051.html (accessed 29 November 2012).

[33]Ibid.

[34]Ibid.

[35]Ibid.

[36]Ibid.

[37]Ibid.

[38]*Al-Aulaqi v. Panetta*, Complaint 1, No. 12-cv-01192, United States District Court for the District of Columbia, 2012.

[39]Ibid., 2.

[40]Ibid.

[41]Ibid., 3.

[42]Ibid.

[43]Ibid.

[44]Ibid., 15-16.

[45]Ibid., 16.

[46]"Death from Afar," *The Economist*, 3 November 2012, 61.

CHAPTER 2

LITERATURE REVIEW

"How is it that judicial approval is required when the United States decides to

target a U.S. citizen overseas for electronic surveillance, but . . . judicial scrutiny is

prohibited when the United States decides to target a U.S. citizen overseas for death?"[1]

"Can the Executive order the assassination of a U.S. citizen without first affording him

any form of judicial process whatsoever, based on the mere assertion that he is a

dangerous member of a terrorist organization?"[2] In *Al-Aulaqi v. Obama*, the District

Court recognized these as "[s]tark, and perplexing, questions" yet failed to address them.[3]

This is not surprising, as American courts have not directly addressed the legality of

drone strikes in general, let alone in the context of the targeted killing of U.S. citizens.

The reluctance of the courts to address these issues stems from the political question

doctrine, which "excludes from judicial review those controversies which revolve around

policy choices and value determinations constitutionally committed for resolution to the

halls of Congress or the confines of the Executive Branch."[4] As noted by the District

Court, "the presence of a political question suffices to prevent the power of the federal

judiciary from being invoked."[5] Fortunately, legal scholars have explored where the

District Court dared not to tread.

In *Targeted Killings: Law and Morality in an Asymmetrical World*, Andrew

Altman provides an overview of targeted killings and the legal and moral issues they

raise.[6] Altman defines targeted killing as "the intentional killing by a state of an

individual identified in advance and not in the state's custody."[7] He describes two main

approaches to assessing the legality and morality of targeted killing: the law-enforcement

9

and armed-conflict models.[8] He explains that these models "provide moral frameworks for judging the actions of governments and determining what the law should be."[9]

According to Altman, proponents of the law-enforcement model argue that governments should deal with terrorism using the same "personnel, procedures, and standards used in responding to any kind of serious crime."[10] He notes that the law-enforcement model "pointedly rejects the idea that the targeted killing of suspected or known terrorists is morally or legally permissible, apart from situations in which the targeted individual poses an imminent (or otherwise unavoidable) threat to the lives of civilians and killing him is the only way to stop the threat from being realized."[11] He further notes that defenders of the law-enforcement model argue that "Excluding such emergency situations, the authorities are morally and legally obligated to capture the suspect and forbidden from killing him."[12]

In contrast, Altman explains that proponents of the armed-conflict model deem the law-enforcement model inadequate to deal with the threat of terrorism.[13] He notes their argument that suspected and known terrorists should be treated as enemy combatants who violate the laws of war by targeting civilians, and "whose threat should be met, in large measure, by military means on the basis of principles appropriately applied during a time of war."[14] He further notes that the armed-conflict model allows states to try suspected terrorists in military rather than civilian courts, and offer them less rigorous due process, because their failure to distinguish themselves from civilians makes them "unprivileged belligerents."[15] Furthermore, Altman maintains that, under the armed-conflict model, individuals do not necessarily need to pose an imminent threat to the lives of others in order to be killed by the state.[16]

In comparing the law-enforcement model to the armed-conflict model, Altman notes that while under the law-enforcement model, an individual can be intentionally killed only as a last resort, when capture is not possible, and the killing is "strictly indispensible to save human life from unlawful attack," under the armed-conflict model, "a legitimate target can be permissibly killed, even if capture would be costless."[17] He states "Only if and when the enemy surrenders is it then forbidden to intentionally kill him."[18]

Altman then examines the application of the law-enforcement and armed-conflict models to the debate over the legitimacy of target killing. Altman observes that:

> One of the notable features of the debate over targeted killing is that each side regards the other as proposing an approach that is not merely sub-optimal but unacceptable. The proponents of the law-enforcement model do not simply say that targeted killing is less than the best way to respond to terrorism; rather they reject it as morally and legally impermissible. On the other side, defenders of the armed conflict model insist that for a state threatened by terrorists to forego the practice, when the state has the requisite means, is an unacceptable abdication of its responsibility to [protect] its citizens.[19]

Altman explains that proponents of the law-enforcement model reject targeted killing as morally and legally impermissible because "they see targeted killings as nothing more than unjustifiable homicide by the state, in other words, as murder by the officials who plan and execute the killings."[20] He notes that these proponents argue that targeted killings violate the targeted individual's right to due process of law.[21] He further notes their argument that targeted killings cannot be justified under the right to self-defense, as the individual targeted often poses no imminent threat to human life.[22]

Altman also explains that proponents of the armed-conflict model regard traditional law-enforcement methods for addressing terrorism as woefully obsolete.[23] He notes that these proponents argue that "suspected and known terrorists are not like other

11

criminal suspects and not even like members of the Mafia and other organized crime enterprises,"[24] in that they often receive clandestine support from purportedly friendly governments that "provide resources such as money, forged documents, weaponry, training camps and safe haven."[25] With regard to self-defense, Altman notes that proponents of the armed-conflict model "reject the idea that the imminence requirement, understood as a demand to wait until an attack is just about to happen, applies to actions taken against the enemy in a time of war."[26] He claims that, according to these proponents, "When a country is at war, it is not required to refrain from lethal action until the next attack from the enemy is on the verge of occurring before launching a strike."[27]

Next, this chapter examines arguments for and against the law-enforcement and armed-conflict models. It demonstrates Altman's argument that "each side regards the other as proposing an approach that is not merely sub-optimal but unacceptable."[28]

In *The Rule of Law at the Crossroads: Consequences of Targeted Killing of Citizens*, Ryan Alford argues against the armed-conflict model. He maintains that allowing the executive branch to impose the death penalty against a U.S. citizen without trial threatens the rule of law.[29] According to Alford, "the thirteenth century was the last time that the executive branch of any common law country, without the involvement of its judicial or the legislative branches, asserted that it was legal to kill a citizen on the basis of an executive order."[30] He explains how in 1282, King Edward II issued an extrajudicial royal order to execute a Welsh noble named Gruffydd ap Llwelyn for treason. The ensuing uproar raised by the other nobles forced the English King to publically reaffirm his commitment to the Magna Carta. He notes that "the targeted

12

killing of Al-Awlaki brings to an end seven consecutive centuries of faithful observance to the Magna Carta's decree that no one be killed by the executive without trial."[31]

Alton compares President Obama's authorization of the targeted killing of Anwar al-Awlaki to King Edward II's royal order to kill Gruffydd . He argues that "if the courts uphold a decision declaring that the president's powers are so broad as to preclude any judicial determination of whether the targeted killing program is prohibited by the Due Process Clause, we stand to lose the benefits of a seven-hundred year old tradition of resistance to arbitrary power."[32]

Alford argues the Constitution prohibits targeted killings.[33] He maintains that "the Framers were particularly concerned with the possibility of this sort of executive punishment of alleged traitors."[34] Alford addresses the Framer's attitudes toward military jurisdiction over treason. Alford takes issue with the notion that al-Awlaki was merely being subjected to military justice pursuant to President Obama's executive orders. Alford argues "the Framers would not have countenance arguments that the president could evade the bar on Bills of Attainder by authorizing an executive death warrant to be executed by the military, since the president cannot order the military to do anything outside the bounds of what Congress has authorized (or can authorize)."[35]

In *Targeted Killing and the Courts: A Response to Alan Dershowitz*, Jameel Jaffer, the Director for the American Civil Liberties Union's (ACLU's) Center for Democracy, echoes Alford's support for the law-enforcement model. Jaffer refutes the Obama Administration's assertion that it has the authority to conduct targeted killings against U.S. citizens without judicial review.[36] Jaffer acknowledges that states may use lethal force against enemy combatants during time of war.[37] Jaffer also acknowledges that government agents may use lethal force "without charge or trial" when necessary as a last resort for self-defense or defense of others.[38] However, Jaffer argues that "the courts have a role to play in articulating the standards under which lethal force is used and in ensuring that the government actually complies with those standards."[39] Jaffer compares this role to that similarly performed by American courts whenever an individual alleges an agent of the government used excessive force.[40] Noting that the executive "must obtain judicial approval to monitor a U.S. citizen's communications or search his briefcase," Jaffer rejects the Obama Administration's apparent argument that the President may execute a U.S. citizen "without any obligation to justify [his] actions to a court or to the public."[41] Jaffer states "While the Constitution designates the President Commander-in-Chief of the nation's armed forces, it does not provide him with a blank check over the lives of its citizens."[42]

However, in *Rebutting the Civilian Presumption: Playing Whack-a-Mole Without a Mallet*, Colonel Mark Maxwell argues that, in the wake of 9/11, the U.S. rightly abandoned the law-enforcement model because it limits the U.S. government's ability to combat terrorism.[43] Maxwell instead favors tailoring the law of war to justify the targeted killing of terrorists under the armed-conflict model.[44] He explains that whereas the law of war currently allows the state to target civilians only while they engage in direct hostilities against the state, his approach would categorize individuals as either nontargetable civilians or targetable belligerents.[45] Maxwell concludes that "while status is paramount in targeting decisions, the determination of status should be based on the individual's pattern of conduct and that pattern must be sufficient to rebut the presumption that the individual enjoys the protected status of a civilian."[46]

Maxwell explains that prior to 9/11, the U.S. regarded terrorism as a matter for domestic law-enforcement.[47] Maxwell notes that the paradigm of law-enforcement treated terrorists as suspected criminals and protected them from lethal force, so long as their conduct did not constitute an unlawful threat to human life.[48] According to Maxwell, this paradigm presumes intentional killing by the state is unlawful unless necessary for self-defense or defense of others.[49] He states, "The law-enforcement paradigm assumes that the preference is not to use lethal force but rather to arrest the terrorist and then to investigate and try him before a court of law."[50] Maxwell states that this paradigm "fails to consider the case of a terrorist who works outside the state that he plans to attack and is virtually immune to arrest for much of the time that he is preparing for the attack, because he is operating in an area of the world where law-enforcement is weak or non-existent."[51] In critiquing this paradigm, Maxwell states:

> This situation is analogous to the game of Whack-a-Mole, but with an additional layer of rules. In this game, if the mole (the terrorist) does not pop up its head (take a direct part in hostilities), then the state may not respond. When the mole does pop up, the amount of force the state can use via its mallet is limited to the minimum force required. And instead of whacking the mole with the mallet, if the state can catch the mole, it must. . . . To make matters worse for the state, the mole operates in places where arrest is remote because governance is weak or non-existent. The law-enforcement paradigm assumes some control over the space in which the state is conducting operations. Little to no control over that space exists in places like Yemen. The game can be played under this paradigm, but the winner is assured: the mole.

He further states "The events of 9/11 demonstrated these weaknesses in the law-enforcement paradigm and led the United States to rethink its approach to terrorism."[52]

Turning his focus away from law-enforcement, Maxwell explains that the law of war authorizes use of lethal force "on the basis of two concepts: the right of self-defense and the right to engage a hostile force as defined by a superior authority."[53] Quoting the

15

Standing Rules of Engagement (SROEs) for U.S. forces,[54] he explains that the right of self-defense encompasses "the authority and obligation to use all necessary means available and to take all appropriate actions to defend th[e] . . . unit and other U.S. forces in the vicinity from a hostile act or demonstration of hostile intent."[55] Maxwell notes that self-defense "hinges on the actions of others; it is based on *conduct*." He describes the right of self-defense as subjective because although the actions of the perceived hostile force might be benign, the soldier might view those actions as a demonstration of hostile intent.[56] Maxwell states that "If the soldier is reasonable in his response, then his response is justified and legal."[57] Contrasting the right of self-defense with the right to engage declared hostile forces, Maxwell notes that soldiers need not observe any hostile act or intent before using lethal force against opposing forces, once a superior authority has declared those forces hostile. Maxwell states that "in other words, the declared hostile force is based on *status*."[58]

Maxwell argues that under the law of war, terrorists may be killed not just in self-defense or in defense of others, on the basis of their conduct but also because of their status as belligerents, as determined by the President under the Authorization for the Use of Military Force.[59] He explains that by declaring war against al-Qaeda and its associated forces, the U.S. subsequently applied the law of war to its actions against these and other terrorist organizations.[60] In contrasting the law-enforcement model to the armed-conflict model, he states:

> Unlike the law-enforcement paradigm, the law of war requires neither a certain conduct nor a reasonable amount of force analysis to engage belligerents. In armed conflict, it is wholly permissible to inflict "death on enemy personnel irrespective of the actual risk they present." Killing enemy belligerents is legal unless specifically prohibited; for example, enemy personnel out of combat, like

the wounded, the sick, or the shipwrecked. A situation of armed conflict negates the law-enforcement presumption that lethal force against an individual is justified only when necessary. If an individual is an enemy, then "soldiers are not constrained by the law of war from applying the full range of lawful weapons. . . ." The soldier is told by the state that an enemy is hostile and may engage that individual without any consideration of the threat currently posed. The enemy is declared hostile; the enemy is now targetable.[61]

Maxwell then addresses how to best tailor the law of war regarding targeted killing to combat international terrorism.[62] According to Maxwell the principal legal question raised by targeting terrorists is "[H]ow can a state determine that an individual is a belligerent, vice a civilian, and therefore a legitimate target under the law of war, just as a combatant is a legitimate target because of his status as a member of an armed force?"[63]

Maxwell describes terrorists as an asymmetric enemy because "they do not wear uniforms or identifiable insignia to distinguish themselves from civilians." Maxwell further notes that "[t]he difficulty with combating an asymmetric enemy has pushed the United States toward a policy of targeted killing." He defines targeted killing as "the use of lethal force by a state or its agents with the intent, premeditation, and deliberation to kill individually selected persons who are not in the physical custody of those targeting them."[64] He explains, states use targeted killing not for judicial or law-enforcement reasons, but rather to eliminate individuals they view as dangerous. Maxwell warns that unless the policy regarding targeted killing is adroitly structured to deal with certain situations, such as targeting U.S. citizens, making targeted killings a favored method of combating terrorists raises the risk that the law of war could be driven in a direction that is unwise for its long term health.[65]

He notes that terrorists seek to look like innocent civilians and purposely blend into the civilian population in order to garner the protection afforded to civilians by the

Geneva Conventions and the law of war.[66] Maxwell notes that in a conflict between two states, otherwise known as an international armed-conflict, an individual may have the status of either a combatant or civilian. He explains that although the law of war allows states to target combatants, it also requires them to protect civilians not directly taking part in hostilities. Maxwell explains that the principle of distinction prohibits attacks against civilians, which he defines as "all persons who are not members of State armed forces or organized armed groups of a party to the conflict."[67]

Maxwell also explains that the requirement for precision further restricts the use of lethal force. He notes that precision requires that the killing be as precise as militarily possible to avoid harming those other than the combatant. He states:

> [D]istinction blurs when non-state actors conduct asymmetric warfare against a state. When a belligerent—someone who is taking hostilities against the state—is not wearing insignia or uniform and is also blending into the civilian population, then precision becomes extremely difficult. The *obligation* of a belligerent is to "comply with the rules of international law applicable in armed conflict. . . ." If the combatant, like a terrorist fails to comply with these rules, then he could forfeit the protections of combatant immunity. . . . But in targeting a belligerent, the assumption is that the state knows that the belligerent, who looks like a civilian, is hostile. The price a belligerent pays for non-compliance is simply a loss of combatant immunity; the state, on the other hand, must now track a threat in an asymmetrical environment where the protection of the civilian population, which is the state's obligation, is in the balance.[68]

Maxwell then turns his attention to the problem of targeting terrorists. He explains that until recently, international law categorized individuals as combatants, who could be targeted, or civilians, who could be targeted only so long as they engaged in hostilities. This effectively insulated terrorists from being continuously targeted. Maxwell notes that in 2009 the International Committee of the Red Cross (ICRC) established a new category: organized armed groups. According to the ICRC, "[i]n non-international armed-conflict, organized armed groups constitute the armed forces of a non-State party

18

to the conflict and consist only of individuals whose continuous function is to take a direct part in hostilities."[69]

Maxwell delineates two requirements for considering an individual a member of an organized armed group. First, he explains that "the individual must be a member of an organized group because the '[c]ontinuous combat function requires lasting integration into an organized armed group.'"[70] Second, he explains that "the organized group must be conducting hostilities."[71]

Maxwell explains that most terrorists can thus be continuously targeted because of their status as members of an organized armed group. However, Maxwell concludes that under the current ICRC guidance "it is questionable whether Mr. al-Awlaki is a member of an organized armed group due to the factual question of whether he has taken direct part in hostilities."[72] Maxwell disagrees with this definition, stating "The test for status must be the *threat* posed by the group and the member's course of conduct which allows that threat to persist."[73] Maxwell proposes a revised definition, delineating three steps for states to take in order to conclude that an individual is targetable based on his status as a member of an organized armed group.[74] First, he explains that "the state must determine whether the group that is combating the state is organized and armed."[75] Second, he explains that "the state must demonstrate that the individual is a member of that group as evidenced by a pattern of conduct which demonstrates a military function."[76] Third, he explains "the state must ensure that the protections of the surrounding civilians are honored when the member of the organized armed group, now a belligerent, is targeted."[77] With regards to al-Awlaki, Maxwell states:

19

Al-Awlaki's status would most likely be different under the revised definition of what entails a member of an organized armed group; his pattern of conduct that he is performing a military function would give him the status of being a member of the group. He is now targetable. This pattern would need to be established through facts that show a military function.[78]

Maxwell concludes that "while status is paramount in targeting decisions, the determination of status should be based on the individual's pattern of conduct and that pattern must be sufficient to rebut the presumption that the individual enjoys the protected status of a civilian."[79]

In *Targeting Anwar Al-Aulaqi: A Case Study in U.S. Drone Strikes and Targeted Killing*, Benjamin R. Farley extends the debate over targeted killings to the facts of the case of Anwar al-Awlaki, arguing that the armed-conflict model justifies his targeted killing. Farley argues that "although both self-defense and armed conflict provide authority for a state's use of force when their respective parameters are satisfied, self-defense fails to justify the continuous targeting of Anwar al-Aulaqi [sic] and other individuals on [the] U.S. targeted killing list."[80] He also argues that "al-Aulaqi [sic] was likely justifiably targetable on a continuous basis due to his direct participation in an ongoing armed-conflict between al-Qaeda in the Arabian Peninsula (AQAP) and Yemen, a conflict in which the United States is intervening."

Farley defines targeted killing as the "intentional, premeditated and deliberate use of lethal force by [a] State . . . or by an organized armed group . . . against a specific individual who is not in the physical custody of the [State employing the targeted killing.]"[81] Citing open sources, Farley notes that the U.S. maintains at least two lists of individuals targeted for killing: a list maintained by the U.S. Military, and a list maintained by the Central Intelligence Agency.[82]

Farley differentiates the right of self-defense under the law-enforcement model with anticipatory self-defense under the armed-conflict model. Farley notes that, as described in the *Caroline* incident, under the law of war, self-defense requires three elements: necessity, proportionality, and immediacy.[83] As explained by Farley, the victim state's use of force must: (1) be necessary to disrupt the harmful attack it faces, (2) be proportional to the harm it faces, and (3) either anticipate an imminent armed attack or immediately follow that attack. Farley goes on to explain that "anticipatory self-defense is lawful in the face of an imminent armed attack but the mere threat of force will not justify self-defense."[84]

Like Maxwell, Farley acknowledges that the principle of distinction protects civilians from being directly targeted "unless and for such time as they take a direct part in hostilities." However, like Maxwell, Farley also acknowledges that "In both international and non-international armed conflicts, civilians who take a direct part in hostilities forfeit their protected status under international humanitarian law while they directly participate in hostilities."[85] He goes on to state "Although there is no precise definition of direct participation in hostilities, it is generally accepted that direct participation in hostilities requires an act that is likely to result in a harm to the adversary; a sufficient causal relationship between the act and the harm; and a nexus between the act and ongoing hostilities."[86]

Unlike Maxwell, Farley claims there is "little doubt that Anwar al-Aulaqi [sic] was directly participating in hostilities—and therefore, a legitimate target." Farley acknowledged that "al-Aulaqi's high profile role as author and producer of AQAP's English-language Inspire magazine does not amount to direct participation in hostilities."

However, he argues that "al-Aulaqi [sic] was not a mere *agent provocateur* but also an operational leader of AQAP." He claims al-Aulaqi's emphasis on attacking the U.S and recruitment of attackers like Umar Farouk Abdulmutallab for the Christmas Day bombing of Northwest Airlines Flight 253 amounts to direct participation in hostilities, and that by directly participating in hostilities, lost the protection accorded to civilians, which made him subject to use of force.

This chapter provided a review of the literature addressing the legality of targeted killing. It provided an overview of the law-enforcement and armed-conflict models, and provided arguments for and against each. This chapter revealed the following gap in the literature. Although legal scholars such as Alford and Jaffer conclude that the law-enforcement model better protects the constitutional rights of U.S. citizens, they fail to consider whether it adequately addresses the asymmetrical threat of terrorism. Similarly, although legal scholars such as Maxwell and Farley conclude the killing of al-Awlaki was legally permissible under the armed-conflict model, they fail to consider whether al-Awlaki's status as a U.S. citizen afforded him any additional protection. Thus, the literature reveals a gap in knowledge about a model that balances the need to protect constitutional rights with the need to address the threat of terrorism. This paper will attempt to fill this gap by first exploring three models proposed by other legal scholars for providing greater due process to U.S. citizens targeted for killing, and ultimately synthesizing a unique national security model, based on national security courts, as proposed by author Glenn Sulmasy, that would be used to adjudicate a citizen's status as a member of an organized armed group, as described by Maxwell. The following chapter explains the methodology for the remainder of this paper.

[1] *Al-Aulaqi v. Obama*, 727 F.Supp.2d 1, 8-54 (D.D.C. 2010).

[2] Ibid., 9.

[3] Ibid., 8.

[4] *Japan Whaling Ass'n v. American Cetacean Soc.*, 478 U.S. 221, 230 (1986).

[5] *Al-Aulaqi v. Obama*, 727 F.Supp.2d 1, 9.

[6] Claire Finkelstein, Jens D. Ohlin, and Andrew Altman, eds. *Targeted Killings: Law and Morality in an Asymmetrical World* (Oxford, United Kingdom: Oxford University Press, 2012).

[7] Ibid., 5.

[8] Ibid.

[9] Ibid.

[10] Ibid.

[11] Ibid., 6.

[12] Ibid.

[13] Ibid.

[14] Ibid.

[15] Ibid.

[16] Ibid.

[17] Ibid.

[18] Ibid.

[19] Ibid.

[20] Ibid., 7.

[21] Ibid.

[22] Ibid.

[23] Ibid.

[24] Ibid.

[25] Ibid., 8.

[26] Ibid.

[27] Ibid.

[28] Ibid., 6.

[29] Ryan Alford, *The Rule of Law at the Crossroads: Consequences of Targeted Killing of Citizens*; 4 Utah L. Rev. 1203, 1206 (2011).

[30] Ibid., 1204.

[31] Ibid., 1206.

[32] Ibid., 1207.

[33] Ibid., 1209.

[34] Ibid.

[35] Ibid., 1219.

[36] Jameel Jaffer, 37; Wm. Mitchell L. Rev. 5315 (2011).

[37] Wm. Mitchell L. Rev. 5317.

[38] Ibid.

[39] Ibid.

[40] Ibid., 5318.

[41] Ibid.

[42] Ibid.

[43] Mark Maxwell, *Rebutting the Civilian Presumption: Playing Whack-a-Mole Without a Mallet?*, in *Targeted Killings: Law and Morality in an Asymmetrical World*, eds. Claire Finkelstein, Jens D. Ohlin, and Andrew Altman (Oxford, United Kingdom: Oxford University Press, 2012), 31.

[44] Ibid. Stating that "the law of war regarding targeted killing can be tailored to combat international terrorism."

[45] Ibid., 34.

[46]Ibid.

[47]Ibid., 33.

[48]Ibid., 36.

[49]Ibid., 37.

[50]Ibid., 36.

[51]Ibid., 37.

[52]Ibid.

[53]Ibid., 31.

[54]Joint Chiefs of Staff, Chairman of the Joint Staff Instruction (CJCSI) 3121.01A, *Standing Rules of Engagement for U.S. Forces* (Washington, DC: Government Printing Office, 15 January 2000), A-3.

[55]Ibid., 31.

[56]Ibid., 32.

[57]Ibid.

[58]Ibid.

[59]Ibid., 38.

[60]Ibid., 33.

[61]Ibid., 38.

[62]Ibid., 33.

[63]Ibid.

[64]Ibid., 32-33.

[65]Ibid., 33.

[66]Ibid., 32.

[67]Ibid., 39.

[68]Ibid., 40.

[69]Ibid., 49.

[70]Ibid., 50. Quoting ICRC Guidance.

[71]Ibid., 51.

[72]Ibid.

[73]Ibid., 55.

[74]Ibid.

[75]Ibid.

[76]Ibid.

[77]Ibid.

[78]Ibid., 58.

[79]Ibid., 34.

[80]Benjamin R. Farley, *Targeting Anwar Al-Aulaqi: A Case Study in U.S. Drone Strikes and Targeted Killing*, 2; Natl. Sec. L. Brief 57, (2012).

[81]Natl. Sec. L. Brief 60.

[82]Ibid., 61.

[83]Ibid., 78.

[84]Ibid., 80.

[85]Ibid., 75.

[86]Ibid., 75.

CHAPTER 3

RESEARCH METHODOLOGY

This research paper will utilize legal analysis as its primary methodology. In particular, it will utilize the "Issue, Rule, Application, and Conclusion" method. Similar to the differential diagnosis used by physicians, the Issue, Rule, Application, and Conclusion method provides a basic methodology for legal analysis. It is the most commonly used approach to answering legal questions in law school and on bar exams. The Issue, Rule, Application, and Conclusion method requires the attorney to state the issue in a way that clearly delineates the subject of controversy, articulate that controversy's governing rule, analyze the facts in light of the law, and draw a reasonable conclusion.[1]

This research paper addresses the following issue: Is the targeted killing of U.S. citizens legal? Although this paper recognizes the controversy surrounding the targeted killing of individuals in general, it specifically focuses on the legal implications of killing U.S. citizens. However, this paper does not limit its analysis to the targeted killing on the battlefield. It also examines the legality of targeted killings in locations where the U.S. Military does not have a continuous presence, and the local government retains some control of the area.

This research paper then articulates two sets of rules that govern targeted killings in general: the law-enforcement and the armed-conflict models. This paper explains that the law-enforcement model requires a state's agents to use ordinary methods and procedures of law-enforcement and justice to control terrorism. This paper also explains that the law-enforcement model allows the agents of a state to kill an individual only

27

when that individual poses an imminent threat of death or serious bodily injury to others, and the circumstances prohibit less lethal means from being used. Conversely, this research paper explains that the armed-conflict model allows a state's agents to kill individuals not only in self-defense, but also based on their status as members of a declared hostile force.

This research paper conducts its analysis of the issue within its scope in the following manner. It applies the facts of the targeted killing of Anwar al-Awlaki to both the law-enforcement model and the armed-conflict model. In doing so, this paper utilizes a series of judicial balancing tests. As defined by *Black's Law Dictionary*, a balancing test is "A judicial doctrine, used esp. in constitutional law, whereby a court measures competing interests—as between individual rights and governmental powers, or between state authority and federal supremacy—and decides which interest should prevail."[2] These balancing tests demonstrate that neither model adequately serves the decision maker when determining whether to pursue the targeted killing of a U.S. citizen. They demonstrate that the law-enforcement model is inadequate because it fails to adequately address threats to national security. They also demonstrate that the armed-conflict model fails to adequately protect the constitutional rights of U.S. citizens. This research paper then analyses three proposals from legal scholars for providing greater protection to the constitutional rights of U.S. citizens targeted for killing. These proposals include judicial review of executive decisions to target U.S. citizens by military judge advocates, appointing personal representatives to advocate on behalf of U.S. citizens targeted for killing during executive agency deliberations, and creating a new judicial court to review and approve targeted killings.

28

This research paper concludes that none of the proposed options adequately balances the need to protect the constitutional rights of U.S. citizens targeted for killing with the need to mitigate threats to national security. This paper further concludes that a third model based on a system of national security courts is needed, to balance the governments interest in countering threats to national security, with the targeted individuals interest in obtaining due process of law.

---

[1]Texas Southern University, "What is IRAC?" www.tsu.edu/pdffiles/academics/ law/life/support/IRAC.pdf (accessed 30 November 2012).

[2]Bryan A. Garner, *Black's Law Dictionary*, 9th ed. (West: 2009).

CHAPTER 4

ANALYSIS

This paper seeks to answer the following research question: Is the targeted killing of U.S. citizens legal? This chapter attempts to answer this question through legal analysis of the facts of the case of the targeted killing of Anwar al-Awlaki under the law-enforcement model and the armed-conflict model. This analysis reveals that neither model justifies his targeted killing.

The law-enforcement model maintains that governments should deal with terrorism using the same "personnel, procedures, and standards used in responding to any kind of serious crime."[1] For U.S. citizens, these include the right to due process before being deprived of life, liberty, or property. From the facts of the case, it appears Anwar al-Awlaki received very little due process before being killed by the government. As the U.S. Government keeps its kill lists classified, he received no official notice of the government's intent to kill him. Moreover, he was never accused of any crime, never given a trial to determine his guilt or innocence, never given an opportunity to confront his accusers or review the evidence against him, and never given the opportunity to speak on his own behalf. Thus, the targeted killing of Anwar al-Awlaki cannot be justified under the law-enforcement model because the government failed to afford him the ordinary level of due process.

The law-enforcement model also "pointedly rejects the idea that the targeted killing of suspected or known terrorists is morally or legally permissible, apart from situations in which the targeted individual poses an imminent (or otherwise unavoidable) threat to the lives of civilians and killing him is the only way to stop the threat from being realized."[2] Attorney General Holder acknowledged the law-enforcement model's imminent threat requirement, when he stated that the targeted killing of a U.S. citizen would be permissible at least when "First, the U.S. government has determined, after a thorough and careful review, that the individual poses an imminent threat of violent attack against the United States; second, capture is not feasible; and third, the operation would be conducted in a manner consistent with applicable law of war principles." However, the government never publicly asserted that al-Awlaki posed any imminent threat. In fact, it appears likely that the government did not even consider whether the threat posed by al-Awlaki was imminent when it ordered his targeted killing. As explained by Dennis Blair, the former Director of National Intelligence, when deciding whether to order the targeted killing of any U.S. citizen, the U.S. Government must merely consider "whether that American is involved in a group that is trying to attack us, [and] whether that American is a threat to other Americans."[3] Mr. Blair's statement notably lacks the law-enforcement model's requirement for an imminent threat in order to justify the killing of an individual by the state. Additionally, the U.S. waited one year from the time al-Awlaki was placed on the targeted kill list to kill him, casting doubt on the imminence of the threat he posed. Thus, the targeted killing of Anwar al-Awlaki cannot be justified under the law-enforcement model because the U.S. failed to prove, or even assert, that he posed any imminent threat to the lives of civilians.

Similarly, under the armed-conflict model, the state may authorize its agents to kill in self-defense or in defense of others, but states may also authorize their agents to kill in defense of property. As the SROEs for U.S. Forces explains "Unit commanders always retain the inherent right and obligation to exercise unit self-defense in response to a hostile act or demonstrated hostile intent." The SROEs define hostile acts authorizing the use of lethal force in self-defense broadly, to include attacks or other uses of force against U.S. persons or property, and include, for example, force used "to preclude or impede the mission and/or duties of U.S. forces, including the recovery of U.S. personnel or vital USG [United States Government] property." Thus, agents of the state may kill in defense of persons or property under the armed-conflict model.

Additionally, unlike the law-enforcement model, the armed-conflict model rejects the idea that an individual must pose an imminent threat, understood as a demand to wait until an attack is just about to happen, in order to take action against that individual in a time of war. Although the SROEs define hostile intent as "[t]he threat of imminent use of force against the United States, U.S. forces or other designated persons or property," they go on to explain that "[i]mminent does not necessarily mean immediate or instantaneous."[4] Accordingly, the armed-conflict model allows anticipatory self-defense. As described in the *Caroline* incident, under the law of war, self-defense requires three elements: necessity, proportionality, and immediacy.[5] In other words, the victim state's use of force must: (1) be necessary to disrupt the harmful attack it faces, (2) be proportional to the harm it faces, and (3) either anticipate an armed attack or immediately follow that attack. Moreover, although anticipatory self-defense is lawful when facing impending harmful attack, the mere threat of force will not justify it.[6]

In the case of Anwar al-Awlaki, the U.S. Government failed to demonstrate that it was necessary to kill him in order to disrupt some harmful attack. Al-Awlaki was killed in Yemen, a country which not only the U.S. was not at war with, but also shared normal diplomatic relations. To that end, the U.S. failed to demonstrate that Yemeni authorities either could not or would not arrest him. Moreover, the U.S. Government failed to demonstrate that killing al-Awlaki was proportional to the harm he posed. As noted by Farley, "In the context of self-defense, proportionality demands that the force used be no more than required to deter or disrupt an impending attack."[7] Again, the U.S. failed to demonstrate that Yemeni authorities either could not or would not arrest him. Finally, the U.S. failed to demonstrate al-Awlaki posed an immediate threat for almost the entire year that he held a place on the targeted kill list, before being killed. In Yemen, al-Awlaki was far from U.S. troops. He was far from U.S. civilian population centers. He was far enough away that the U.S. had to use remotely piloted drones to find him. Based on the information publicly available, it appears just as likely that al-Awlaki was merely hiding, rather than being on the verge of mounting some harmful attack. Thus, the targeted killing of Anwar al-Awlaki cannot be justified as anticipatory self-defense under the armed-conflict model because the U.S. failed to prove that his killing was necessary and proportional, to avoid or disrupt a threatened attack.

However, the armed-conflict model also allows states to kill individuals not only on the basis of self-defense, but also on the basis of status. As explained by Maxwell, members of the U.S. Military may use lethal force against a potential adversary either when invoking their right of self-defense, based on that potential adversary's conduct, or their right to engage a hostile force as declared by a superior authority, based on that potential adversary's status. As Maxwell states "The soldier is told by the state that an enemy is hostile and may engage that individual without any consideration of the threat currently posed. The enemy is declared hostile; the enemy is now targetable." In the current conflict, the authority of the state to declare forces hostile stems from the

Authorization for the Use of Military Force, in which Congress authorized the President to "use all necessary and appropriate force against those nations, organizations, or persons he determines planned, authorized, committed or aided the terrorist attacks that occurred on September 11, 2001, or harbored such organizations or persons, in order to prevent any future acts of international terrorism against the United States by such nations, organizations or persons."[8]

The SROEs reflect the President's ability to declare particular organizations and individual persons hostile under the Authorization for the Use of Military Force. They define a Declared Hostile Force to include "Any civilian, paramilitary, or military force, or terrorist that has been declared hostile by appropriate U.S. authority." According to the SROEs, "Once a force is declared hostile by appropriate authority, U.S. forces need not observe a hostile act or demonstrated hostile intent before engaging the declared hostile force." The *U.S. Army Operational Law Handbook* explains that this is because the basis for engagement shifts from conduct to status. The handbook makes clear that individuals, as well as organizations, can be declared hostile. It states, "Once a force or individual is identified as a DHF, the force or individual may be engaged, unless surrendering or *hors de combat* [meaning "outside the fight"] due to sickness or wounds." Moreover, since the individual has been declared hostile, and no demonstration of act or intent is necessary, members of a declared hostile force are subject to continuous targeting. For example, an enemy soldier may be killed by an airstrike while sleeping in his barracks, even when not actively participating in hostilities on the battlefield, because that soldier has been declared hostile by an appropriate superior authority, usually stemming from a declaration of war or similar legislation.

34

Combatants provide the most concrete example of individuals that can be declared hostile. As defined by international law, combatants include all members of the armed forces of a party to a conflict. As noted above, combatants can be continuously targeted even when not actively participating in hostilities. In contrast, civilians can be targeted only when actively participating in hostilities. Until recently, international law recognized only combatants and civilians. In other words, individuals were either members of the armed forces, who could be continuously targeted, or not. International law made no distinction between individuals such as terrorists, who are not members of the armed forces of any state, and civilians. In 2009, however, the ICRC established the category of an organized armed group, which it defines as "the armed forces of a non-State party to the conflict and consist only of individuals whose continuous function is to take a direct part in hostilities." While at first glance, this definition is no broader than that of civilians who participate in hostilities, the ICRC's guidance explains that "The crux of distinguishing whether an individual is a member of an organized armed group or a civilian, which includes a civilian participating in hostilities, is whether the person performs a continuous combat function."[9] In other words, while individuals such as Judge Advocates, for example, may not continuously take part in hostilities, they undoubtedly perform a continuous combat function and are therefore targetable on a continuous basis.

However, Maxwell makes clear that "Non-state actors should be targeted only if membership in the organized armed group can be positively established by the state through a pattern of conduct demonstrating a military function."[10] Maxwell states "It is the obligation of the state—in this case, the United States—to establish the facts:

35

al-Awlaki's degree of involvement in the Fort Hood rampage; the degree of support and aid he gave to Abdulutallab in the attempted Christmas Day airliner attack; and his other attempts to use violence against the United States and his functions within those efforts." Maxwell argued al-Awlaki's involvement in these events made him a belligerent and therefore a legitimate target.[11] In contrast, Farley believed Anwar al-Awlaki directly participated in hostilities, because he claimed al-Awlaki was an operational leader within al-Qaeda. Both Maxwell and Farley's analysis would make al-Awlaki a legitimate target under the armed-conflict model, but they fail to consider whether al-Awlaki retained any constitutional protections.

While it seems clear that U.S. citizens can be killed on the battlefield as members of a declared hostile force, it remains unclear what form of due process they must be afforded. The following three articles consider this issue, and offer escalating methods and legal procedures for protecting the due process rights of individuals targeted for killing.

In "My Fellow Americans, We Are Going to Kill You: The Legality of Targeting and Killing U.S. Citizens Abroad," Mike Dreyfuss rejects the application of the law-enforcement model to targeted killings in general but recognizes that the armed-conflict model requires additional protection of the constitutional rights of U.S. citizens. He examines how the U.S. Government could conduct targeted killings in accordance with international law, while also adhering to domestic due process protections, afforded to all U.S. citizens.

Dreyfuss differentiates targeted killing from assassination and execution. He defines targeted killing as "a state's intentional and premeditated use of lethal force through agents acting under color of law against a specific, reasonably unobtainable individual." Dreyfuss's definition differs from Altman's definition of targeted killings in that Dreyfuss emphasizes that a state's agents must act under color of law. Dreyfuss differentiates target killings from assassinations by explaining that, while assassinations are politically motivated, targeted killings are based strictly on security concerns. He explains that while a series of executive orders prohibit assassination, they do not prohibit the killing of individuals who have military importance in time of war. Dreyfuss also differentiates target killings from executions by explaining that while execution requires extensive due process and judicial review, targeted killing are extrajudicial because the individual targeted has made himself unobtainable. He notes "The government reserves targeted killings for individuals of military significance who cannot be brought to justice by other means." Dreyfuss maintains:

> The federal government may target and kill individuals who have not been convicted of crimes, because targeted killing and execution serve different purposes. Execution is a punishment for a crime. Targeted killing is not a punishment. It is a military strike. The state does not intend to right a wrong but to further a military objective. Viewed in this light, prior judicial review of targeted killings—like prior judicial review of military decisions to kill enemies (U.S. citizens or not) on the battlefield—is unnecessary.

Dreyfuss then opines why the law-enforcement model does not apply to targeted killings. He notes that in its Memorandum in Support of Plaintiff's Motion for a Preliminary Injunction for Al-Aulaqi v. Obama, the ACLU argued that targeted killings were lawful only where the individual targeted posed a concrete, specific, and imminent threat of death or serious physical injury. Dreyfuss further notes that the ACLU supports its argument with a standard taken from domestic case law limiting a Law Enforcement Officer from using deadly force to apprehend a suspect where the suspect poses no immediate threat to the officer or others. Dreyfuss disagrees with the ACLU's argument. He maintains that the domestic law enforcement standard applied by the ACLU does not apply to targeted killing because the purpose of targeted killing differs from the purpose of law enforcement. Dreyfuss states:

> Most importantly, the purpose of killing is different. In the cited cases [by the ACLU], the police may use lethal force to protect themselves and others from the immediate threat that the suspect poses and not from future operations that the suspect is preparing. If the purpose is to protect the citizenry from an immediate threat, but there is no immediate threat, then killing by domestic law-enforcement is not permissible. The purpose of a targeted killing is to protect citizens from an attack that is being prepared, where waiting until the threat is temporally immediate is not feasible.

Although Dreyfuss rejects the application of the law-enforcement model to targeted killings in general, Dreyfuss maintains that some of the model's requirements do apply in the case of targeted killing of U.S. citizens. Dreyfuss argues U.S. citizens deserve greater protection from targeted killing than noncitizens. He recognizes that the Bill of Rights applies extraterritorially, and that the U.S. "cannot strip its citizens of constitutional protection merely because they are not present in the country."

Dreyfuss explains that U.S. citizens have the right to trial by jury when accused of a crime. He notes that levying war against the U.S., or giving aid and comfort to enemies of the U.S., constitutes the crime of treason. In applying the facts of Anwar Al-Aulaqi's case, Dreyfuss concludes that "Al-Aulaqi [sic] was, by his own words and as demonstrated through his actions, levying war against the United States." He explains "Al-Aulaqi [sic] advocated for, participated in, and recruited others to participate in war. . . . Under the qualifications for treason, he was not only an adherent to an enemy but also a leader within an enemy organization, al-Qaeda." Because of this, Dreyfuss believed al-Awlaki made a prime candidate for conviction of treason, because by serving as one of its principal recruiters and scholars, he gave aid and comfort to al-Qaeda. However, Dreyfuss makes clear that under the Constitution, conviction of treason requires a trial. Additionally, Dreyfuss notes the Constitution also requires competent evidence from at least two witnesses, or a confession from the accused traitor "in open court." Dreyfuss argues "If the government plans to treat a citizen as a traitor, then the government must give the citizen notice that he is wanted for the crime of treason." He explains that "Without notice, the accused lacks the opportunity to avail himself of his constitutional right to stand trial before a jury of his peers." Although Dreyfuss faults the government for not giving al-Awlaki notice of its intent to treat him as a traitor, noting the difference between execution, the punishment for conviction of treason, and targeted killing, a state's response to military threat, Dreyfuss states "With regard to targeted killings, the Constitution, however, does not demand that a person who is a military threat to the United States remain at large because he is good at avoiding arrest."

Accordingly, Dreyfuss then turns his attention to the due process necessary to label a U.S. citizen a military threat. Dreyfuss also explains that U.S. citizens are guaranteed the right to procedural due process when facing deprivation of a private interest by a government agency. He states "The U.S. Supreme Court articulated the standard for evaluating agency compliance with procedural due process in Matthews v. Eldridge." Dreyfuss notes that Eldridge established the following three part balancing test:

> First, a court will consider the private interest that will be affected by the official action. Second, it will consider the risk of an erroneous deprivation of such interest through the procedures used and the probable value, if any, of additional or substitute procedural safeguards. Third it will consider the government's

interests, including the function involved and the fiscal and administrative burdens that the additional or substitute procedural requirements would entail.

Citing the reasoning in *Hamdi v. Rumsfeld*, Dreyfuss suggests that the Eldridge test would also apply to targeted killings. Dreyfuss maintains that a government agency, such as the Central Intelligence Agency, would be responsible for making the decision to kill any U.S. citizen. He notes that "When an agency makes a binding decision on the rights of a particular party by reference to historical facts, it is conducting an adjudication." He argues the presumed procedures used by the government in selecting U.S. citizens for targeted killing fall short of the Eldridge test. Quoting Congressional testimony by Dennis Blair, the former Director of National Intelligence, Dreyfuss explains that when deciding whether to order the targeted killing of any U.S. citizen, the U.S. Government must merely consider "whether that American is involved in a group that is trying to attack us, [and] whether that American is a threat to other Americans." Noting that the private interest at stake involves the life of a U.S. citizen, and that the risk of erroneous deprivation is quite great, Dreyfuss argues that "the killings should not be undertaken haphazardly or without consideration of the available evidence." As called for by the Eldridge test, Dreyfuss then considers additional or substitute procedures. Dreyfuss acknowledges that trial by jury affords U.S. citizens the greatest protection from erroneous deprivation of a private interest, such as an individual's life, and believes the government would offer trial by jury to any U.S. citizen suspected of terrorism, with the caveat the individual must first be willing to surrender to law-enforcement authorities. Dreyfuss then considers trial in absentia, but rejects the idea because "A trial in absentia would be incredibly costly, in terms of the expenditure of state resources and in terms of the opportunity cost of not attacking the target when expedient." Additionally, noting the difficulty of obtaining and working with classified information, Dreyfuss states "an Article III-style trial will have greatly limited access to evidence as compared with an agency's initial determination."

Dreyfuss argues targeted killings of U.S. citizens could be lawful where the targeted citizen receives notice and an opportunity for a hearing, followed by a Judge Advocate General determination of his decision not to avail himself of further process, and of his permissibility as a military target. Drefuss states "This would balance the target's interest in his life against the threat he poses to the lives of his fellow Americans."

In "Ready . . . Fire . . . Aim! A Case for Applying American Due Process Principles Before Engaging in Drone Strikes," Carla Crandall argues for invocation of American due process principles before commencement of a drone strike in order to ensure their legitimacy. Crandall explains "This approach rests on the Fifth Amendment to the U.S. Constitution, which provides, in relevant part, that the U.S. government shall not deprive any person of life 'without due process of law.'" She argues that "the Supreme Court has offered signals as to the procedural safeguards that may be due those individuals whom the United States wishes to target with a drone." She posits that "though Hamdi v. Rumsfeld and Boumediene v. Bush do not signal a mandate for full-scale criminal proceedings before a drone assault is undertaken, these cases do suggest that the executive may be required to afford some level of ex ante process to ensure their legitimacy." She notes that in *Hamdi v. Rumsfeld*, the Supreme Court held that "U.S. citizens detained by the government have the right to both notice as to the basis for detention, and a meaningful opportunity to challenge their detention before a neutral

41

decision-maker." She notes that the degree of due process afforded is based on consideration of three factors:

> First, the private interest that will be affected by the official action; second, the risk of an erroneous deprivation of such interest through the procedures used, and the probable value, if any, of additional or substitute procedural safeguards; and finally, the Government's interest, including the function involved and the fiscal and administrative burdens that the additional or substitute procedural requirement would entail.

According to Crandall, Hamdi and Boumediene demonstrate that "American due process does not necessitate standard full-scale criminal proceedings of this ilk when the exigencies of war dictate that something less can be employed." She states "The key, however, is that this lesser degree of process must ultimately still operate to prevent the arbitrary 'exercise of governmental power.'" Crandall concludes that in light of the Obama Administration's exponentially increased reliance on targeted killings to prosecute the war on terror, "it is imperative that the U.S. government adopt procedures that enable it to operate in a manner consistent with its values and principles—for '[i]t would indeed be ironic if, in the name of national defense, we would sanction the subversion of one of those liberties . . . which makes the defense of the Nation worthwhile.'" (Quoting Hamdi). She states "Though American due process may likewise independently fail to provide a wholly satisfactory answer as to the legality of drone strikes, its application at a minimum provides another basis for ensuring their legitimacy." She believes "Hamdi and Boumediene signal that whatever process is adopted must comply with the Mathews balancing test." Crandall suggests "given that the individuals listed on the U.S. strike list are subject to unlimited military force, the government arguably ought to be required to prove before a tribunal that listed persons are in fact legitimate drone targets." Crandall recognizes "it may indeed be unreasonable for a terrorist himself to appear before a tribunal to challenge his status as a legitimate drone target." However, she believes "it does not appear unreasonable to require the executive to develop internal procedures affording a limited parallel." She suggests "In order to ensure that the government is in fact meeting its burden of proof, however, the executive could appoint an ombudsman or personal representative with advocacy responsibilities for each potential drone target."

In "Bouncing the Executive's Blank Check: Judicial Review and the Targeting of Citizens," Samuel Adelsberg argues the targeted killing of U.S. citizens should require a basic level of judicial process. Adelsberg goes much further than Dreyfuss, who calls for a Judge Advocate General legal review, or Crandall, who advocates appointing an ombudsman or personal representative, to protect the due process rights of U.S. citizens targeted for killing. Adelsberg "calls for the creation of a circumscribed court to adjudicate, ex ante, the legality of targeting operations in specific cases where there is prior knowledge that the target is a U.S. citizen." In other words, he proposes creating courts specifically to adjudicate the targeted killing of U.S. citizens.

Adelsberg begins with a review of the protections afforded to U.S. citizens. He explains that the Fourth Amendment prohibits the extrajudicial killing of any individual by law enforcement officials, or other agents of the government, unless that individual poses significant imminent danger to those officials or other individuals. Adelsberg also explains that the Fifth Amendment's Due Process Clause protects individuals from deprivation of life, liberty, or property without due process of law. Like Crandall, Adelsberg notes that in *Hamdi v. Rumsfeld*, the Supreme Court held that "due process required Hamdi [as a U.S. citizen] to have a meaningful opportunity to challenge his

43

enemy combatant status." Additionally, Adelsberg notes the Court's assertion that "Hamdi was entitled to 'notice of the factual basis for his classification, and a fair opportunity to rebut the Government's factual assertions before a neutral decisionmaker.'" Noting that due process applies extraterritorially, Adelsberg maintains that "The relevance of these precedents to the targeting of citizens is clear: the constitutional right to due process is alive and well—regardless of geographic location."

Adelsberg argues that "in light of the protections the Constitution affords U.S. citizens, there must be a degree of inter-branch process when the government targets such individuals." Adelsberg maintains an inter-branch process between the executive and judiciary is necessary because "[t]he current intra-executive process afforded to U.S. citizens is not only unlawful, but also dangerous," because the executive is not a neutral decision-maker. Noting a potential conflict of interest when executive agencies like the Department of Defense and the Central Intelligence Agency are tasked with making decisions about targeting U.S. citizens for killing, Adelsburg points out that "the goal of those charged with targeting citizens like al-Awlaki is not to strike a delicate balance between security and liberty but rather, quite single-mindedly, to prevent attacks on the United States." He maintains that "in the realm of targeted killing, where the deprivation is of one's life, the absence of any 'neutral decision-maker' outside the executive branch is a clear violation of due process guaranteed by the Constitution."

Adelsberg argues the level of due process currently afforded to U.S. citizens targeted for killings, falling entirely under the Executive Branch, falls short of that envisioned under the Constitution. However, he recognizes the difficulties and disadvantages associated with providing traditional criminal trials for suspected terrorists operating overseas. Thus, Adelsberg advocates creating a Citizen Targeting Review Court (CTRC).

Adelsberg describes the CTRC as a specialized court created to adjudicate claims against U.S. citizens suspected of terrorism by the government, before the government may proceed with targeted killing. He cites bankruptcy, patents, copyright, tax, and international trade courts as examples of specialized courts created for adjudicating particularly complex issues, requiring unique knowledge that already exists in the federal system. Adelsberg proposes modeling the CTRC on the Foreign Intelligence Surveillance Court (FISC), "which was created by the Foreign Intelligence Surveillance Act (FISA) to provide a statutory framework for the use of electronic surveillance in the context of foreign intelligence gathering." He notes that the FISC functions in the following manner:

The government must come before the FISC, which is comprised of federal judges, and seek approval for electronic surveillance, physical searches, pen registers, trap and trace devices, or orders for production of tangible things anywhere within the U.S. under Foreign Intelligence Surveillance Act. Proceedings before the FISC are *ex parte* ["by one party"] and non-adversarial. The court hears evidence presented solely by the Department of Justice. The FISC is structured so as to operate "as expeditiously as possible" given the time sensitivity of surveillance operations.

Adelsberg maintains that "The CTRC would function in a similar manner to the FISC, thereby providing the targeted killing analysis with neutral and detached oversight." He explains:

Were the executive branch to target a citizen, it would need to present its reasoning to a CTRC judge. This judge would be a Senate-confirmed Article III judge with prior national security expertise to appreciate the military concerns brought about by this added level of process. The CTRC judges would issue opinions to establish standards and to guide future decisions. Barring opposition from the executive branch, redacted versions of these opinions would be released to the public.

However, contrary to the FISC's non-adversarial model, Adelsberg proposes appointing expert Federal or Military Defense Counsel, as approved by the Chief Justice of the Supreme Court and with the necessary security clearances, to represent the interests of the citizen targeted, as guardians *ad litem*. Adelsberg maintains that "[t]he government would be required to turn over to the accused's defense attorney any exculpatory intelligence regarding the targeted citizen." However, Adelsberg argues that, because of the risk of tipping off a potentially dangerous terrorist to U.S. intentions, actual notice of the proceeding to any U.S. citizen suspected of terrorism should not occur.

Adelsberg explains the CTRC would provide judicial oversight in two phases: (1) the General Targeting Phase, and (2) the Situational Targeting Phase. He argues that during the General Targeting Phase, the government would have to establish that an individual posed an ongoing threat to the U.S., thus meriting targeted killing. According to Adelsberg, "The government must demonstrate that (1) the citizen targeted either is 'part of' or provided 'substantial support' to al-Qaeda, the Taliban, or associated forces; (2) the citizen target is operational and actively engaged in planning, commanding, or carrying out attacks on the United States; and (3) the threat posed by the citizen target's action is imminent." He argues that because this proceeding involves the life of a U.S. citizen, "[t]he most fitting standard for this type of adjudication would be the 'beyond a reasonable doubt' standard in criminal law." During the Situational Targeting Phase, Adelsberg would require the executive to certify the legality of the targeted killing before the CTRC *ex post*, and suggests the executive would have to demonstrate, *inter alia*, the infeasibility of capture. Adelberg explains the Situational Targeting Phase "must be post facto, because real-time judicial oversight in the form of an Article III judge making the ultimate decision would be a significant encroachment on the executive's ability to execute a war as Commander-in-Chief, in addition to being logistically problematic."

Adelsberg also argues for an emergency targeting mechanism, based on the Foreign Intelligence Surveillance Act's emergency order provision. He explains the Attorney General may authorize the immediate targeted killing of a U.S. citizen where the Attorney General:

1. Reasonably determines that an emergency situation exists with respect to the individual being targeted.

2. Reasonably determines that the factual basis for the issuance of an order exists, in that the target would have been approved through the General Targeting Phase.

3. Informs a CTRC judge at the time of such authorization that the decision has been made to target this U.S. citizen.

4. Reports back to the CTRC judge within seven days with the justification for the operation.

In applying the facts of Anwar al-Awlaki's case to the model, Adelsberg argues that the CTRC would find that al-Awlaki merited target killing because he provided substantial operational support to al-Qaeda, as established by his connections to the Fort Hood shooter, and the Christmas Day bomber, and posed an imminent threat to the U.S.

In addressing the type of process due to U.S. citizens targeted for killing, Adelsberg states "Due process guarantees more than classified memos exchanged between executive branch lawyers. It guarantees a substantive check on the executive branch before it targets one of its own citizens."

In general, Dreyfuss, Crandall, and Adelsberg agree that the targeted killing of U.S. citizens requires some form of due process, however, they disagree as to what type and how much. Nonetheless, even minimal due process demands notice and an opportunity to be heard.

As stated earlier, al-Awlaki received no official notice of the government's intent to kill him. More significantly, the government afforded al-Awlaki no opportunity to be heard. As the Supreme Court noted in *Hamdi*, due process requires allowing U.S. citizens a meaningful opportunity to challenge the decision of an executive agency before a neutral decision maker. As explained, trial by jury affords U.S. citizens the best opportunity to be heard. However, although criminal convictions require trial by jury, an administrative adjudication by an executive agency does not. The amount and form of due process may vary. As explained by Attorney General Holder, "The Constitution guarantees due process, not [necessarily] judicial process."

However, as the Supreme Court noted in *Hamdi*, due process does require a neutral decision maker. Although Crandall's proposal would require the executive to develop internal procedures affording internal review of decisions to target U.S. individuals, and suggests appointing an ombudsman or personal representative to ensure the government meets its burden of proof, her proposal falls short because it lacks a neutral decision maker from outside the executive branch.

As stated earlier, American courts have not directly addressed the legality of the targeted killings of U.S. citizens overseas. The issue of due process was raised in *Aulaqi v. Obama* by Anwar al-Awlaki's father. However, as the district court noted, it is unlikely any court established under Article III of the U.S. Constitution[12] ever will, because of the political question doctrine.

It is well established that Article III courts have no authority to review political questions.[13] Under the political question doctrine, courts lack jurisdiction to decide cases that address nonjusticiable political questions.[14] The political question doctrine "excludes from judicial review those controversies which revolve around policy choices and value determinations constitutionally committed for resolution to the halls of Congress or the confines of the Executive Branch."[15]

In *Baker v. Carr*[16] the United States Supreme Court established the following indicia for determining whether a case presented a political question:

> [1] a textually demonstrable constitutional commitment of the issue to a coordinate political department; or [2] a lack of judicially discoverable and manageable standards for resolving it; or [3] the impossibility of deciding without an initial policy determination of a kind clearly for nonjudicial discretion; or [4] the impossibility of a court's undertaking independent resolution without expressing lack of the respect due coordinate branches of government; or [5] an unusual need for unquestioning adherence to a political decision already made; or [6] the potentiality of embarrassment from multifarious pronouncements by various departments on one question.[17]

A case presents a nonjusticiable political question where the court finds any one of the aforementioned *indicia* present.[18]

The political question doctrine has blocked civilian courts from considering a great many issues involving the military. For example, private military contractors have achieved success by arguing that courts lack jurisdiction to hear tort liability claims against them under the political question doctrine.[19] However, it's unlikely al-Awlaki will be the last U.S. citizen targeted for killing. According to the Council on Foreign Relations, "The number of terror incidents involving Islamic radicals who are U.S. citizens has seen an uptick in recent years."[20] Thus, there will remain a need to adjudicate the rights of U.S. citizens. Nonetheless, there remains other forums open for affording due process to individuals targeted for killing.

Military commissions are one such forum. Their use to try U.S. citizens for violations of the law of war has been deemed constitutional by the Supreme Court.

In *Ex Parte Quirin*, the Supreme Court considered whether the U.S. Government could detain a group of German saboteurs, accused of violating the law of war, for trial by military commission. Although all of the saboteurs were born in Germany, the group included one U.S. citizen named Herbert Hans Haupt, whose parents emigrated to the U.S. from Germany when he was five years old and became naturalized citizens. Haupt returned to Germany prior to 1941, and after the declaration of war with the U.S., received sabotage training at a school near Berlin, Germany. Haupt then boarded a German submarine at a seaport in Occupied France, which carried him and three other saboteurs across the Atlantic with orders to destroy U.S. war industries and facilities. Haupt and his fellow saboteurs came ashore at Ponte Vedra Beach, Florida on or about 17 June 1942 wearing German uniform caps and carrying explosives. After burying their uniforms and equipment, they proceeded in civilian clothes to Jacksonville, Florida. When agents of the Federal Bureau of Investigation later took them into custody, they had in their possession substantial sums of U.S. currency handed to them by an Officer of the German High Command.

On 2 July 1942, President Franklin D. Roosevelt appointed a military commission to try Haupt and the other attempted saboteurs' petition for *habeas corpus*. The petitioners contended the President lacked authority to order their trial by military tribunal. They claimed the Fifth and Sixth Amendments entitled them to trial by jury in civilian courts. The group sought to file petitions for *habeas corpus* in the District Court for the District of Columbia. The District Court denied their request, and the group appealed the district court's decision through to the Supreme Court.

The government argued that "The law of war embraces citizens as well as aliens (enemy or not); and civilians as well as soldiers are all within their scope." The government further argues that "Indeed it was for the very purpose of trying civilians for war crimes that military commissions first came into use."

The Supreme Court affirmed the denial of the attempted saboteurs request to file petitions for *habeas corpus* in the District Court. The Supreme Court concluded the Commission had jurisdiction to try the petitioners. The Supreme Court noted Congress authorized trial of those charged with relieving, harboring or corresponding with the enemy, either by court martial or military commission, in the Articles of War. The Supreme Court stated "We conclude that the Fifth and Sixth Amendments did not restrict whatever authority was conferred by the Constitution to try offenses against the law of war by military commission, and that petitioners, charged with such an offense not required to be tried by jury at common law, were lawfully placed on trial by the Commission without a jury." The Supreme Court made a distinction between lawful and unlawful combatants, stating "Lawful combatants are subject to capture and detention as prisoners of war by opposing military forces." It also stated that although unlawful combatants are also subject to capture and detention, they are also subject to trial and punishment by military tribunals for acts which render their belligerency unlawful.

In *Ex Parte Quirin*, the Supreme Court made clear that U.S. citizenship does not preclude trial by military authorities for violations of the law of war. However, legislation passed since *Ex Parte Quirin* makes trial by military authorities unlikely.

Although the Supreme Court allowed the trial of a U.S. citizen by military commission in *Ex Parte Quirin*, Attorney General Holder believes that, "by statute, military commissions cannot be used to try U.S. citizens." The Military Commissions Act of 2006 "establishes procedures governing the use of military commissions to try alien unlawful enemy combatants engaged in hostilities against the United States for violations of the law of war and other offenses triable by military commission." It defines an "alien" as "a person who is not a citizen of the United States."

The Military Commissions Act also likely precludes implementation of Dreyfuss's proposal, whereby targeted killing of U.S. citizens could be lawful where the targeted citizen receives notice and an opportunity for a hearing, followed by a Judge Advocate General determination of his decision not to avail himself of further process, and of his permissibility as a military target. Although not strictly a military commission, having one's status determined by a Judge Advocate General does constitute adjudication by military authorities, which runs contrary to the intent of the Military Commissions Act.

Read narrowly, the Military Commissions Act of 2006 limits the trial of U.S. citizens for violations of the laws of war, to civilian courts. However, that reading assumes only military and civilian options, and fails to consider hybrid solutions offered by other legal scholars.

In the National Security Court System, Glenn Sulmasy calls for the creation of national security courts. Sulmasy believes that although military commissions are permissible as a matter of law, "as a matter of policy, they are inappropriate for trying unlawful belligerents in the current armed conflict."[21] Sulmasy states "To date, the advocacy has essentially been divided into two camps:

1. Those who view the conflict with al Qaeda as requiring a law-enforcement response and thus civilian courts and the due process ordinarily accorded to U.S. citizens.

2. Those who view the conflict as an armed-conflict, believing the law of war paradigm to be appropriate for handling the detainees.

Sulmasy recognizes that while the military law construct has not met America's needs, we must also refrain from retreating to the policies of the purely law-enforcement model. Sulmasy argues "both the military commissions and the civilian system have failed to best meet the need of policy makers and those employed to protect the national security." Sulmasy explains neither military commissions nor the civilian system are equipped to properly strike the balance of military law, intelligence needs, human rights obligations, and the need for justice—both perceived and actual."[22] Sulmasy maintains "That since the al Qaeda fighter is a hybrid of a warrior and an international criminal; the war itself is a hybrid of traditional armed conflict and law enforcement operations; thus it logically follows that we need a hybrid court—a mix of our Article III courts and the existing military commissions."[23]

Sulmasy proposes Congress create a National Security Court System under its Article I, Section 8 Powers. Article I, Section 8 gives Congress the power "To constitute Tribunals inferior to the Supreme Court." Sulmasy envisions a National Security Court System will have jurisdiction over citizens and noncitizens alike. Sulmasy believes "it is important for the system to not distinguish between citizen and noncitizen when handling alleged al-Qaeda fighters." Sulmasy states "The oversight of the National Security Court must be performed by the Department of Justice National Security Division."

A CTRC, as described by Adelsberg in the literature review, could also serve as such an alternate forum. However, I argue that a National Security Court (NSC), as described by Sulmasy would be superior for the following reasons. First, a NSC would have jurisdiction over citizens and noncitizens alike. Thus, it could be used to adjudicate claims from both detainees at Guantanamo Bay and individuals on the U.S. government's targeted killing list. The multipurpose nature of the NSC directly addresses one of the criticisms of the CTRC addressed by Adelsberg "that a court that only adjudicates targeted killings would taint the entire judicial system."[24] Additionally, because a NSC would be an Article I rather than an Article III Court, it would avoid the political question doctrine. The very purpose of the NSC would be to deal with political questions. Finally, the NSC would be superior because it would better balance the competing interests of the law-enforcement and armed-conflict models. Although the Adelsberg proposes an emergency targeting mechanism, the CTRC remains heavily reliant on the law-enforcement model, and unduly limits the U.S. government's ability to combat terrorism.

As described by Adelsberg, in order to authorize the targeted killing of a U.S. citizen, the CTRC would require the government to demonstrate that the individual targeted posed an ongoing threat to the U.S. He states, "The government must demonstrate that; (1) the citizen targeted either is 'part of' or provided 'substantial support' to al-Qaeda, the Taliban, or associated forces; (2) the citizen target is operational and actively engaged in planning, commanding, or carrying out attacks on the U.S.; and (3) the threat posed by the citizen target's action is imminent."[25] Adelsberg would also require the executive to certify the legality of the targeted killing before the CTRC *ex post*, and suggests the executive would have to demonstrate, *inter alia*, the infeasibility of capture.[26] These statements demonstrate Adelsberg's heavy reliance on the law-enforcement model. Adelsberg limits his analysis to the law-enforcement model's mandate that the targeted killing of suspected terrorists is legally permissible only in self-defense, when the targeted individual poses an imminent or otherwise unavoidable threat to the lives of others, and killing him is the only way to stop the threat from being realized. He fails to recognize the well established rule under the armed-conflict model that individuals may be targeted for killing on the basis of their status alone. He fails to recognize that Anwar al-Awlaki could have been targeted not just on the basis of self-defense for posing an imminent threat to the lives of others, but also on the basis of his status as a member of an organized armed group for performing a continuous combat function within al-Qaeda.

Additionally, Adelsberg argues that because targeted killing proceedings involve the life of a U.S. citizen, "[t]he most fitting standard for this type of adjudication would be the 'beyond a reasonable doubt' standard in criminal law."[27] Again, Adelsberg relies heavily on the law-enforcement model, failing to recognize that individuals are selected for target killing not as punishment for any particular crime, such as treason, which requires trial by jury or confession in open court, but rather because they pose a threat to U.S. national security interests as members of a terrorist organization. The NSC would not hear criminal cases against U.S. citizens. The court would simply adjudicate whether the U.S. citizen demonstrated conduct sufficient to classify that individual as a member of an organized armed group, allowing him to be continuously targeted, as Maxwell explains, for performing a continuous combat function. As the proceeding would be adjudicatory rather than criminal in nature, the burden of proof should be preponderance of the evidence, rather than beyond a reasonable doubt. Alternatively, if the individual desired a higher burden of proof, that individual could always surrender to law enforcement authorities for trial in ordinary court.

Notably, the CTRC, as described by Adelsberg lacks any requirement for providing notice to the individual targeted. This lack of notice appears to violate the spirit of the Supreme Court's holding in *Hamdi* that "U.S. citizens detained by the government have the right to both notice as to the basis for detention, and a meaningful opportunity to challenge their detention before a neutral decision-maker." Extrapolating the Court's holding to targeted killings, it would seem necessary for any U.S. citizen targeted for killing to receive notice of such action, in order for that individual to have a meaningful opportunity to challenge their targeting. For that reason, the NSC should provide notice in order to meet the demands of minimal due process. Additionally, by providing notice, the NSC would lessen the possibility of authorizing the targeted killing of the wrong individual in error.

A NSC would bridge the gap between the armed-conflict model and the law-enforcement model. Applying the facts of al-Awlaki's case to this proposed national security model, the government would simply have to demonstrate that he performed a continuous military function for al-Qaeda in order to target him for killing. Al-Awlaki would enjoy the presumption that he held the protected status of a civilian, which the government would have to rebut with evidence based on his pattern of conduct. The court would consider evidence presented by the government that al-Awlaki recruited members for al-Qaeda, and assisted with preparations for the bombing of airliners. As in the CTRC, al-Awlaki would have *ad-litem* representatives appointed to protect his due process rights. Instead of a jury, a three judge panel would weigh the evidence, and could reasonably determine that al-Awlaki performed a continuous military function for al-Qaeda, giving him status as a member of an organized armed group, and justifying his targeting under the armed-conflict model. This proceeding would also satisfy the requirement for due process under the law-enforcement model, by providing him with notice and an opportunity to be heard.

---

[1] Ibid.

[2] Ibid., 6.

[3] Ibid., 258.

[4] Ibid., 77.

[5] Farley, 78.

[6] Ibid., 80.

[7] Ibid., 84.

[8] S.J.Res. 23--107th Congress: Authorization for Use of Military Force. (2001).

[9] Maxwell, 50.

[10] Ibid., 55.

[11]Ibid., 35.

[12]Art III states "The judicial Power of the United States, shall be vested in one supreme Court, and in such inferior Courts as the Congress may from time to time ordain and establish."

[13]*See Marbury v. Madision*, 5 U.S. 137, 170 (1803), "Questions, in their nature political, or which are, by the constitution and laws, submitted to the executive, can never be made in this court."

[14]*Occidental of Umm al Qaywayn, Inc. v. A Certain Cargo of Petroleum*, 577 F.2d 1196, 1203 (5th Cir. 1978).

[15]*Japan Whaling Ass'n v. American Cetacean Soc.*, 478 U.S. 221, 230 (1986).

[16]369 U.S. 186 (1962).

[17]*Baker v. Carr*, 369 U.S. 186, 217 (1962).

[18]Ibid., 217.

[19]See *Smith v. Halliburton*, No. H-06-0462, 2006 WL 2521326 (S.D.Tex. Aug. 30, 2006), concluding the court lacked jurisdiction because the case presented a nonjusticiable political question; *Whitaker v. Kellogg, Brown, & Root, Inc.*, 444 F.Supp.2d 1277 (M.D.Ga. July 6, 2006), holding the political question doctrine precluded the court from addressing the issue in the case.

[20]Toni Johnson, http://www.cfr.org/terrorism/threat-homegrown-islamist-terrorism/p11509, last updated 30 September 2011.

[21]Glenn Sulmasy, *The National Security Court System: A Natural Evolution of Justice in an Age of Terror* (New York: Oxford University Press, 2009), 195.

[22]Ibid., 175.

[23]Ibid., 197.

[24]Samuel S. Adelsberg, "Bouncing the Executive's Blank Check: Judicial Review and the Targeting of Citizens," *Harvard Law & Policy Review* 6 (2012): 457.

[25]Ibid., 448-449.

[26]Ibid., 439.

[27]Ibid., 450.

CHAPTER 5

CONCLUSIONS AND RECOMMENDATIONS

This research paper sought to answer the following research question: Is the targeted killing of U.S. citizens legal? It explored two sets of rules governing targeted killings in general: the law-enforcement and the armed-conflict models. It explained that the law-enforcement model requires a state's agents to use ordinary methods and procedures of law-enforcement and justice to control terrorism, and allows state agents to kill only when an individual poses an imminent threat of death or serious bodily injury to others, and the circumstances prohibit less lethal means from being used. Conversely, this paper explained that the armed-conflict model allows state agents to kill individuals not only in self-defense, but also based on their status as members of a declared hostile force.

This research paper analyzed the facts of the targeted killing Anwar al-Awlaki under both the law-enforcement and armed-conflict models. This analysis revealed that neither model justified his targeted killing because he was not afforded adequate due process. Thus, based on evidence available from unclassified and open source material, his killing was likely a violation of al-Awlaki's constitutional rights. However, the targeted killing of U.S. citizens can be justified where they are given notice and a meaningful opportunity to challenge their classification as members of an organized armed group, such as al-Qaeda. This research paper then analyzed three proposals from legal scholars for providing greater protection to the constitutional rights of U.S. citizens targeted for killing. These proposals included judicial review of executive decisions to target U.S. citizens by military judge advocates, appointing personal representatives to

59

advocate on behalf of U.S. citizens targeted for killing during executive agency deliberations, and creating a new judicial court to review and approve targeted killings.

This research paper concluded that none of the proposed options adequately balanced the need to protect the constitutional rights of U.S. citizens targeted for killing, with the need to mitigate threats to national security, revealing a gap in legal scholarship regarding this subject. This paper also concluded that a third model based on a system of national security courts was needed to balance the governments interest in countering threats to national security, with the targeted individuals interest in obtaining due process of law.

The national security model, based on a system of national security courts, provides decision makers with the best basis from which to determine the permissibility of conducting targeted killings against U.S. citizens. As proposed, this national security model avoids the restrictions of the political question doctrine and allows for adequate protection of due process rights for U.S. citizens. This model accomplishes this by linking Sulmasy's proposal for a national security court, with Maxwell's proposal of targeting individuals based on their performance of continuous combat functions. For purposes of targeted killings, this court would adjudicate a U.S. citizens status as a member of an organized armed group, and using a preponderance of the evidence standard, provide legal justification for the use of lethal force.

However, this will require the U.S. Military to make some changes to the way it collects intelligence. Affording U.S. citizens targeted for killing the process due to them under the Constitution will require the military collect intelligence that could be used to demonstrate, in court, that the individual performed a continuous military function within an organized armed group. Such functions should not be limited to the realm of combat arms. Support functions, such as planning and recruitment, should rightly be considered also.

Additionally, this paper focused on targeted killing by military forces only. There are additional legal issues that must be worked through when targeted killings are conducted by civilian agencies, such as the Central Intelligence Agency.

This paper presented a proposal for affording greater due process to the targeted killing of U.S. citizens. As noted by President Obama, although U.S. citizens may represent a threat to the U.S., any process to address that threat must be "subject to the protections of the constitution and due process."[1]

----

[1]"Death from Afar," *The Economist*, 3 November 2012, 61.

BIBLIOGRAPHY

Adelsberg, Samuel S. "Bouncing the Executive's Blank Check: Judicial Review and the Targeting of Citizens." *Harvard Law & Policy Review* 6 (2012): 437-457.

Alford, Ryan P. "The Rule of Law at the Crossroads: Consequences of Targeted Killing of Citizens." *Utah Law Review* 4 (2011): 1203-1273.

Berger, J. M. *Jihad Joe: Americans Who go to War in the Name of Islam*. Dulles, VA: Potomac Books, 2011.

———. "The Myth of Anwar al-Awlaki." *Foreign Policy,* 10 August 2011. http://www.foreignpolicy.com/articles/2011/08/10/the_myth_of_anwar_al_awlaki (accessed 29 November 2012).

Crandall, Carla. "Ready... Fire... Aim! A Case for Applying American Due Process Principles Before Engaging in Drone Strikes." *Florida Journal of International Law* 24 (April 2012): 55-89.

Dreyfuss, Mike. "My Fellow Americans, We Are Going to Kill You: The Legality of Targeting and Killing U.S. Citizens Abroad." *Vanderbilt Law Review* 65, no. 1 (2012): 249-292.

Farley, Benjamin R. "Targeting Anwar Al-Aulaqi: A Case Study in U.S. Drone Strikes and Targeted Killing." *American University National Security Law Brief* 2, no. 1 (2012): 57-87.

Finkelstein, Claire, Jens D. Ohlin, and Andrew Altman, eds. *Targeted Killings: Law and Morality in an Asymmetrical World*. Oxford, United Kingdom: Oxford University Press, 2012.

Jaffer, Jameel. "Targeted Killing and the Courts: A Response to Alan Dershowitz." *William Mitchell Law Review* 37 (2011): 5315-5319.

Joint Chiefs of Staff. Chairman of the Joint Staff Instruction (CJCSI) 3121.01A, *Standing Rules of Engagement for U.S. Forces*. Washington, DC: Government Printing Office, 15 January 2000.

Maxwell, Mark. *Rebutting the Civilian Presumption: Playing Whack-a-Mole Without a Mallet?*. In *Targeted Killings: Law and Morality in an Asymmetrical World*, edited by Claire Finkelstein, Jens D. Ohlin, and Andrew Altman, 31-59. Oxford, United Kingdom: Oxford University Press, 2012.

PBS NewsHour. PBS television broadcast, 30 September 2011. http://www.pbs.org/ newshour/bb/terrorism/july-dec11/awlaki1_09-30.html (accessed 29 November 2012).

Spiro, Peter. "al-Awlaki and Citizenship." *Opinio Juris*, 3 October 2011.
    http://opiniojuris.org/2011/10/03/al-awlaki-and-citizenship/ (accessed 29
    November 2012).

Sulmasy, Glenn. *The National Security Court System: A Natural Evolution of Justice in
    an Age of Terror*. New York: Oxford University Press, 2009.

U.S. Army. The Judge Advocate General's Legal Center and School. *Operational Law
    Handbook.* Charlottesville, VA: USA TJAGLCS, 2012.